EAGLES

BIRDS OF PREY

BY NATHAN SOMMER

EPIC

BELLWETHER MEDIA • MINNEAPOLIS, MN

EPIC BOOKS are no ordinary books. They burst with intense action, high-speed heroics, and shadows of the unknown. Are you ready for an Epic adventure?

This edition first published in 2019 by Bellwether Media, Inc.

No part of this publication may be reproduced in whole or in part without written permission of the publisher. For information regarding permission, write to Bellwether Media, Inc., Attention: Permissions Department, 6012 Blue Circle Drive, Minnetonka, MN 55343.

Library of Congress Cataloging-in-Publication Data

Names: Sommer, Nathan, author.
Title: Eagles / by Nathan Sommer.
Description: Minneapolis, MN : Bellwether Media, Inc., 2019. | Series: Epic.
    Birds of Prey | Audience: Age 7-12. | Audience: Grade 2 to 7. | Includes
    bibliographical references and index.
Identifiers: LCCN 2018003575 (print) | LCCN 2018006812 (ebook) | ISBN
    9781626178786 (hardcover : alk. paper)| ISBN 9781681036243 (ebook)
Subjects: LCSH: Eagles–Juvenile literature. | Birds of prey–Juvenile
    literature.
Classification: LCC QL696.F32 (ebook) | LCC QL696.F32 S66 2019 (print) | DDC
    598.9/42–dc23
LC record available at https://lccn.loc.gov/2018003575

Editor: Kate Moening   Designer: Josh Brink

Printed in the United States of America, North Mankato, MN.

TABLE OF CONTENTS

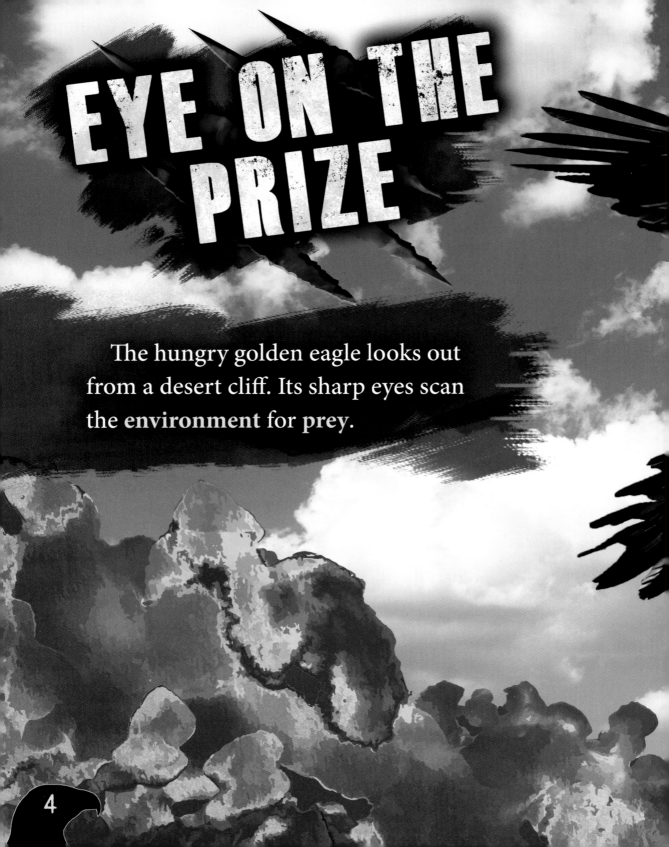

EYE ON THE PRIZE

The hungry golden eagle looks out from a desert cliff. Its sharp eyes scan the **environment** for prey.

The eagle quickly spots a hare more than 1 mile (1.6 kilometers) away.

The powerful **predator** flies closer.
It tracks the hare's every move. Then, it
attacks by surprise!

The golden eagle uses sharp **talons** to carry
its catch back to the cliff. Its hooked beak
tears the prey apart. Dinnertime is here!

WHAT ARE EAGLES?

STELLER'S SEA EAGLE

Eagles are among the largest birds of prey. Some weigh up to 20 pounds (9 kilograms)! Their **wingspan** can be up to 8 feet (2.4 meters) long.

BATELEUR EAGLES

These strong birds have some of the world's best eyesight.

Hunting Buddies

Eagles hunt with humans in parts of Asia. People train the eagles to catch food for them in these areas!

There are more than 60 kinds of eagles. They live on every **continent** except Antarctica.

These birds often prefer to live in large, open areas near bodies of water. They are **apex predators** in their **habitats**.

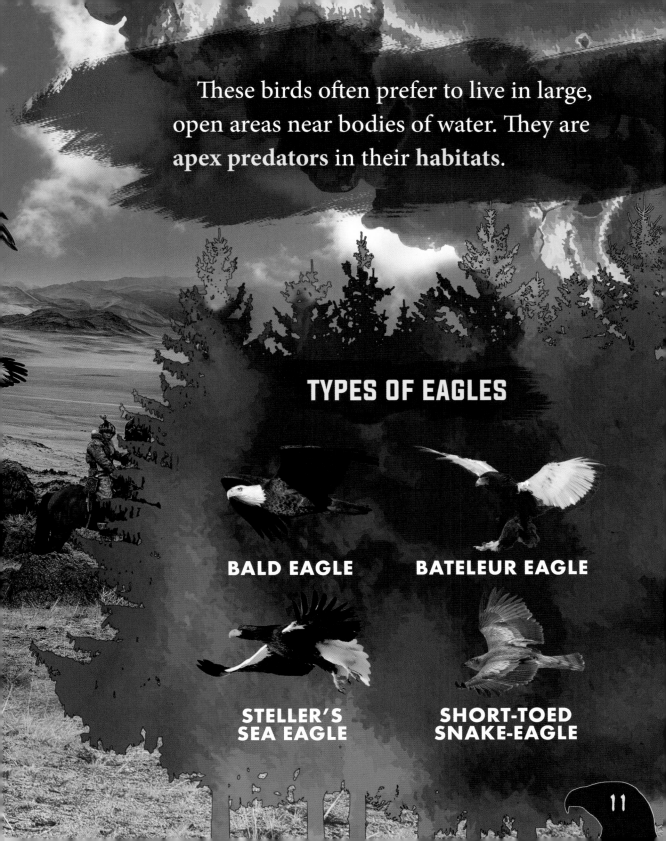

TYPES OF EAGLES

BALD EAGLE

BATELEUR EAGLE

STELLER'S SEA EAGLE

SHORT-TOED SNAKE-EAGLE

HUNTERS OF MANY

Eagles hunt during the day. Fish and small land animals are their favorite foods.

WHITE-TAILED EAGLE

The **carnivores** use different hunting methods for different kinds of prey. The strongest eagles take down deer and goats!

Eagles stay low and slow when hunting large prey. They **stalk** meals before attacking at just the right moment!

14

Water Wings
Some eagles also hunt prey in water. If a catch is too big, they row it into shore with their wings!

Eagles drop from the sky quickly to grab small prey. Their talons are too strong for most.

The Strongest Vision

An eagle's eyesight is five times better than a human's!

Eagle eyes have millions of **cones**. These help spot the tiniest details. Some can see prey more than 2 miles (3.2 kilometers) away!

Their eyes are deep and flat. This lets them see a much clearer picture than other animals.

EAGLE EYES

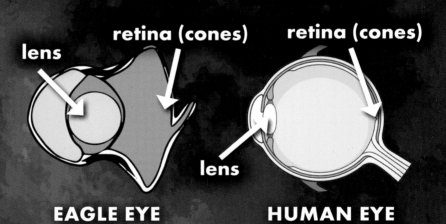

lens

retina (cones)

retina (cones)

lens

EAGLE EYE

HUMAN EYE

Instead of teeth, eagles eat with thick, hooked beaks. These point downward to easily tear apart prey.

HARPY EAGLE

HOOKED BEAK

Their wide mouths take in big chunks of food. These predators rarely go hungry!

BALD EAGLE PROFILE

RED LIST STATUS: **LEAST CONCERN**

LEAST CONCERN	NEAR THREATENED	VULNERABLE	ENDANGERED	CRITICALLY ENDANGERED	EXTINCT IN THE WILD	EXTINCT

AVERAGE LIFE SPAN: **20-30 YEARS**

GREATEST HUNTING TOOL: **VISION**

WINGSPAN: **UP TO 8 FEET (2.4 METERS)**

TOP SPEED: **UP TO 100 MILES (161 KILOMETERS) PER HOUR**

BALD EAGLE RANGE MAP

BALD EAGLE
RANGE =

PREY

PRAIRIE DOGS	RABBITS	SNAKES	FISH

GLOSSARY

apex predators—animals that do not have any natural predators

carnivores—animals that only eat meat

cones—cells in the eye that help see color and small details

continent—a very large mass of land; there are seven continents in the world.

environment—the natural surroundings of an area

habitats—the homes or areas where animals prefer to live

predator—an animal that hunts other animals for food

prey—animals that are hunted by other animals for food

stalk—to follow slowly and quietly

talons—the sharp claws of eagles and other birds of prey

wingspan—the distance between the tip of one wing to the other

TO LEARN MORE

At the Library

Leighton, Christina. *Golden Eagles*. Minneapolis, Minn.: Bellwether Media, 2017.

Statts, Leo. *Eagles*. Minneapolis, Minn.: Abdo Zoom, 2018.

Waxman, Laura Hamilton. *Bald Eagles: Prey-Snatching Birds*. Minneapolis, Minn.: Lerner Publications, 2016.

On the Web

Learning more about eagles is as easy as 1, 2, 3.

1. Go to www.factsurfer.com.

2. Enter "eagles" into the search box.

3. Click the "Surf" button and you will see a list of related web sites.

With factsurfer.com, finding more information is just a click away.

INDEX

The images in this book are reproduced through the courtesy of: Piotr Krzeslak, front cover; Michael G. Mill, p. 2; Paolo-manzi, pp. 4-5; Michele Aldeghi, p. 6 (eagle); Dennis Jacobsen, p. 6 (rabbit); Zoonar GmbH/ Alamy, p. 7; Sergey Uryadnikov, p. 8; Buddy Jenssen, p. 9; Chanwit Whanset, p. 10; DMS Foto, p. 11 (top left); Simone Janssen, p. 11 (top right); Wang LiQiang, p. 11 (bottom left); sbw18, p. 11 (bottom right); Andrew Astbury, p. 12; Krasula, p. 13; Vytautas Knyva, p. 14; Rostislav Stach,p. 15; Stefano Ventur, p. 16; Alexander_P, p. 17 (right); Alfredo Maiquez, p. 18; Michal Ninger, p. 19; Manamana, p. 20; John De Winter, p. 21 (left); hfuchs, p. 21 (left, middle); Jay Ondreicka, p. 21 (right, middle); Karel Bartik, p. 21 (right).